THE LITTLE BLUE DINOSAUR

Kardason Rawandzi

Mayhara Ferraz

tellwell

Tellwell Talent

www.tellwell.ca

ISBN
978-0-2288-2356-8 (Hardcover)
978-0-2288-2357-5 (Paperback)

CRACK,
SNAP,
CRUNCH
The eggs are
all hatching.

Look at these
dinosaurs matching.

Three dinosaurs look around,
Three dinosaurs stomp around,
Three dinosaurs shake the ground.

"But wait," cries a dinosaurs,
"who is this,
Yet to hatch?"

With a nudge and a budge and a shake and a wiggle...
The little dinosaurs begin to giggle.

CRACK, SNAP, CRUNCH
The little egg is hatching.

Oh no, he isn't matching!

"Wah, wah, wah,"
cries the little blue dinosaur.
He isn't the same.

"I want to be
big, red, and tall.
Not small, blue, and lame."

He doesn't have BIG teeth that go
CHOMP, CHOMP, CHOMP.

He doesn't have HUGE feet that go
STOMP, STOMP, STOMP.

He doesn't have a STRONG head that goes
SMASH, SMASH, SMASH.

He doesn't have a LONG
tail that goes
SPLASH,
SPLASH,
SPLASH.

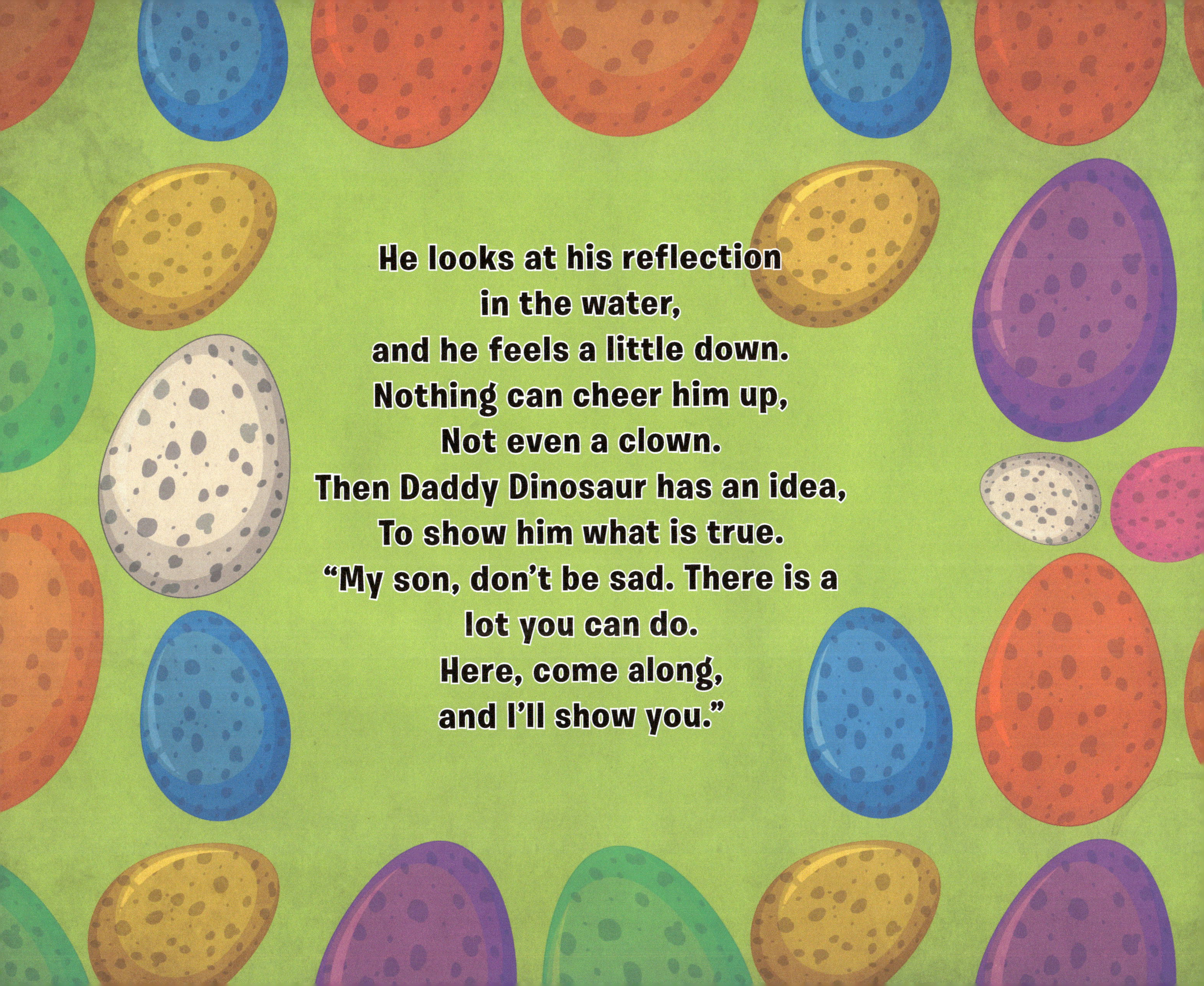

He looks at his reflection
in the water,
and he feels a little down.
Nothing can cheer him up,
Not even a clown.
Then Daddy Dinosaur has an idea,
To show him what is true.
"My son, don't be sad. There is a
lot you can do.
Here, come along,
and I'll show you."

"You are small which means you can fit in tight spaces."

"Your little feet mean you
can win all the races."

"You are blue which means you can hide in many places."

"Your little claws
mean you could
pull silly faces!"

"You can have oodles of fun with
your sisters and brother."

"You will always be loved very much by your mother."

Even though he wasn't
BIG, RED, and
TALL

Being the little blue
dinosaur wasn't so bad,
After all.